SEEING SIGHTS

By the Same Author

In Daylight (Printed Matter, 1995)
Monumenta Nipponica (Saru, 1995)
The Painting Stick: Poems 1991–2002 (Pine Wave, 2005)
From the Japanese (Isobar, 2013)
World Without (Isobar, 2015)

Seeing Sights

1968–1978

Paul Rossiter

ISOBAR PRESS

First published in 2016 by

Isobar Press
Sakura 2-21-23-202, Setagaya-ku,
Tokyo 156-0053, Japan
&
14 Isokon Flats, Lawn Road,
London NW3 2XD, United Kingdom

http://isobarpress.com

ISBN 978-4-907359-17-1

© Paul Rossiter, 2016
All rights reserved.

Acknowledgements

Some poems have previously been published
in NOON: *journal of the short poem* and *World Haiku*;
earlier versions of a few other poems appeared in *In Daylight*
(Printed Matter Press, 1995). Cover photo by Paul Rossiter;
author photo by Armorel Weston.

CONTENTS

I

Seafarer   11

II

Angkor   17
Jantar Mantar Observatory   18
Keep Heading North   19
Work in the Garden   20
Bare Rock   21
Alpine   22
Climbing Rock   23
Uses of the Seashore   26

III

Prelude   31
E. P. Young and Old   32
Visiting Wei Pa after Twenty Years *(Du Fu)*   33
Mad Song   34
Village Idiot   35
In the Mountains: Four Poems   36
In the Mountains: Five Days   39
On Trevose Head   42
Wythburn Valley   43
Musica Universalis   45
Wintering   46

Crossing the Pass	47
Hebridean	48
Gulf Stream	49
Stramongate Bridge, 1 A.M.	50
The Gate	51

IV

Hearing the Great Northern Divers Call	55
Taking the Day Off to Visit the Pound Exhibition	58
Looking at the Work Ken Wall Does	61
Snow Falling and Then Stopping	63
Watching a Documentary about Eihei-ji, Thinking of Gary Snyder	65
Hitch-Hiking to Cornwall, Visiting Grandpa in Hospital, Hitch-Hiking Back Again	68
Starting the Day	74

V

Du Fu *(Armand Robin)*	79
Seeing Sights in Sanctuary Wood	80
The Temptation of St Anthony	82

i.m.

Jo Sawbridge

1945–1970

I

Seafarer

after the Old English

I

And now I fashion a tale of my travels,
iron-hard days when my blood
beat like a hammer, and brine-bitter sorrow
drenched this rib-shackled ache of a heart.

Cold afflicted my limbs and numbed them
when, fettered by frost at boat's prow,
I spent all the eye-straining night-watch
flinching near spray-flecked cliffs.

Wine-flushed, pride-flushed,
rooted among kin on the flourishing earth,
how can a landsman know of a winter
passed on the paths of the sea?

The roar of the ocean,
the slamming of waves on the hull –
and at times the call of a swan,
a gannet's cry or curlew's whistle:
these became for me the laughter and song
of gathered kin in a fire-lit hall –
the clamour of gulls my mead.

Hail showers flew.
Storms beat on the high stone cliffs.
Nesting kittiwake, icy-feathered eagle,
flung their cries on the wind.

2

The shadow of night grows dark on the land.
Snow from the north. Grains of hail
fall on the frost-gripped earth.

No haven on land for a life
blown to tatters by winter gales.

Troubled by thoughts of towering seas,
I hear the creak of tackle
as desire to set forth floods through my heart
in a welter of salt spray and tides.

3

In this valley by the shore, spring
clouds trees with blossom, scatters
a light snowfall of flowers on the fields.

In the wind I hear the whisper of the sea,
and coming over the meadows
the cuckoo's lament,
heralding summer and singing of grief.

A gull cries as it wheels in flight,
and imagination sheds the land like a coat
as it wings to whale-haunted seas, travels
the turning, tide-pulled world
until, unquenched, it comes home
to roost in my heart again.

4

Broken roofs, shattered walls, heaps
of weed-buckled masonry, stones crumbling
beneath winter's white lace of frost.
Age undermined them, grassed them over,
both buildings and builders; and others
now live by the windswept barrows,
bowed down by their dreams as they toil.

We soon turn a corner and meet
old age, look in a mirror one morning
and are ambushed by grey hair,
greying face and failing sight.

What use placing gold in a brother's grave?
No rite or observance will lighten the night
of a body that tastes neither sweetness nor pain,
stirs no limb, ponders nothing,
no thought scurrying in the empty skull.

5

A wave of the sea,
a ripple of wind in downland grasses.

Spring night, creak of tackle,
hawsers cast off from the wharf;
harbour lights flicker on water
as the boat lifts its prow to greet
the first wave beyond the harbour's mouth,
and Orion standing tiptoe on the horizon's line.

II

Angkor

I am a stone temple sunk in the deep-water light of the jungle. Carved gods and goddesses, kings, queens, maidens and armies: the friezes sing on my skin.

Tree roots probe and prise my body apart, the slow violence of the centuries stone by stone displacing and tearing down all the works of man – until I am inhabited by landscape.

Now I know how it is for the elephant and the gnat, for the water turning the irrigation wheels and for the thirsty earth, for the wind, trees, stones and snakes, and for the monkeys who lope and quarrel through the upper branches in sunlight.

I am a clot of leaf-mould on the jungle floor, dreaming of a splintered goddess carved in dancing stone.

Jantar Mantar Observatory

Axis of the earth, equator's line,
phases of the moon, time all round the globe –
an eighteenth-century de Chirico
built them here in brick and stone.

Calendars and calculators,
planes and curves in salmon-coloured brick,
fluted pillars, a small coliseum,
a pink-stuccoed staircase going nowhere –

a surrealist's village square, set down
among palm trees and parched grass
where children scamper
and young men lounge in groups and laugh.

A hot night; swirls of blossom;
leaves crackle under my feet as I walk.
The constellations are racing away from us
in a *kalpa*-long explosion,

but the sky above Jai Singh's garden of astronomy
moves without fault.
The planet spins in space.
The stars sail heaven on their perfect courses.

Keep Heading North

Island Lake, Cross Lake, Sandy Lake —
keep heading north
in boots and furs against the wind,

face pinched by frost, tramping through snow.
Takiyuak Lake, Nonacho Lake —
the English fades, and then gives out.

A white-haired, white-bearded man,
who came from England in his youth,
sits now with his pipe in a house

and tells us how, fifty years ago,
he fell asleep beneath a pine and dreamt
of two moose crossing a snowfield.

(There comes a point, the old trail lost,
when what you used to know
peters out in endless lakes and pine.)

He woke and saw
what he'd just been dreaming:
two moose making their way across

the brilliant, nameless snow.

Work in the Garden

prune and clip
and weed,
train rambling plants

I have no
mind
to impose intention on

these natural things;
myself
grows here:

the garden
uses
what skill I've got

to teach the
heart
how not to grasp

Bare Rock

1

Poured out in lava, or bedded down
grain by filtering grain in prehistoric seas,

pressured, shifted sideways
by the planet's wrinkling crust,

scratched and scraped by glaciers,
worn smooth by water, split by frost:

time itself in the waver of its grain,
in its rough and smooth, its hard and soft.

2

Crossing a pass in late afternoon light,
pitching a small tent at sunset,

busy with guy ropes and sleeping bags
among slabs, boulders and scree;

as the light fails we heat water
over a bud of hissing blue flame,

and sit at ease, leaning our backs against
five hundred million years of stone.

Alpine

1

mountain silence

boulders, sunlit scree
feet pick their own way through

2

stony summit

one blue flower in a cranny

a petal of sky

3

a gap in the cloud
blue tarn

a thousand lonely feet below

Climbing Rock

> *it is thought that beyond this point*
> *it would be impossible to retreat*
> (Climbing guidebook)

1

Move up, peer round – the rope
snakes down through space behind.

All the complicated act
of strength and human balance
keeps you here, toes poised
on half-inch ledges, fingers
probing rock for cracks and faults
and little incut holds

so rock can let you past.

2

Watching rock: an art.

Sometimes it seems to breathe –
holds grow bigger as you gaze,
shrink when seen through fear.

Keep looking until you see the way.

3

Step left on little flakes, reach around
to find the hidden hold – an awkward step –
bridge out across the groove –

your life depends
(the crux just up ahead)

on gravity, which keeps you here
but will kill you if you fall.

4

Legs stretched to their limits,
fingers wrestling with the crack,
one good handhold, but beyond my reach,
there's no way out or off,

I *must* go up!

One small pinch-grip
and a sloping pressure hold
is what I have to get me there:

feet higher, friction on sheer rock,
arms and legs
trembling from the strain –

got it!
pull up, quickly jam that crack –

made it – up and over,
high and trembling on a ledge.

5

Belay to a spike,
take in the rope, see again
sunlight, cloud-shadow
flow over crags and scree.

The rope snakes down through space.
Another two pitches yet.

Climbing!

A shout floats up from below
as my second
starts to make his move

up towards the Move.

Uses of the Seashore

1

Lark's twitter, rise and fall;
lapwings tumble in the air;
slow, in creeks, all day,
shelducks feed in pairs.

2

Slender wings, forked tails,
terns fly dancing out to sea to dive
for little wriggling silver fish
caught in small sharp beaks.

3

Glittering sunlight, distant sea;
a stiff-legged flock
of dunlins probes the low-tide sand-flats –

all take off at once –

a flickering cloud of wings
that veers above the water's edge
then spirals down to feed again.

4

Sitting cross-legged in the dunes
by a windblown driftwood fire.
Sunset fades to starlight. The tide scrolls in,
printing tomorrow's script of ripples on the sand.

III

Prelude

a drawing of attention
a paring down
a glacier's leavings
a standing stone

a tilling of a field
a making of an inhabitation
a seed within a husk
an invention of community

a summoning of powers
a knocking on a wooden door
a song from outside four walls

a message from beyond a frontier
an unpredicted naming
a greening tree

E. P. Young and Old

a cat among the pigeons
polemics
literature put to rights
green eyes, sharp red pointed beard –
knew Kensington stone by stone

Piazza San Marco,
white-haired among the pigeons

> *'it isn't so, not strictly so,
> that's the trouble . . .'*

that I lost my centre fighting the world…

> *– You ordered this for me?
> – Yes, Ezra, eat it.*

tempus tacendi, let the light speak

a bone-white sky
pale brown and yellow marsh grass,
a cold wind ruffles the reed beds at Torcello

Visiting Wei Pa After Twenty Years

after Du Fu

fresh-cut green spring chives
        still wet from the rainy darkness,
fresh boiled rice and yellow millet

        each night
        Scorpio rises as Orion sets

but tonight we've slipped past fate
and sit sharing the light of this lamp

you fill my cup again and again

        'we don't meet so often'

half our friends are dead,
their ghosts cry out in our hearts

        twenty years
        a friendship lasting twenty years

tomorrow
the mountains will be between us

once again
travelling different paths

Mad Song

I gave my wits away:
they made a rotten staff.
In the dark wood, in the thicket,
I dance a tangled dance.

They came, they watched,
they asked me who I am.

I am dream, I said –
cloudless mirror, star-filled sky;
I gaze all night and never wink,
the full moon is my eye.

And I am weather, I topple trees
and beat the harvest flat;
the rain's my flail,
a hurricane under my hat.

Hold him down, they said,
put chains and bars behind those eyes.

In the dark wood, in the thicket,
I hear my tangled cry;
I gnaw my nothing to the bone
and munch my mumble pie.

Village Idiot

the poem is dumb,
it points speechlessly at the world
of which it is a part

       and which masters it
       with strangeness

and it is reduced to
penury
by the shock of that meeting

       the trees are huge
       damp living creatures

the river rushes
between its banks from all its sources

In the Mountains: Four Poems

November

days are short and cold
mountains turn gaunt and bare
the moon moves through its quarters in the frosty sky

    the tide of darkness floods
    down from the pole towards December

the tarn will freeze from shore to shore

    an eyelid blinks

moonlight on a snowy hill

Empty House

hoarfrost on roadside grasses
ice crystals on sheep's droppings

snowflakes melt on the tongue
boots squeak on frozen earth

a dry-stone wall
whistles through its lichened teeth

white fell-tops ache in the sky

    six senses
    a sword of ice

an empty house beneath the wind

It All Becomes Clear Sky

one day we'll just lock up and leave

slates and rafters fall
in windy attics

    no one there to care

green grass along the path
broken garden gate

    bodies disperse
    to moorland earth

a wisp of cloud in a high northern wind

Entering

standing under
the fringe of the last pine

beyond
the last gate

in the steep
valley loud with its beck

the path leading
off through bracken

to mountains
beyond mountains

In the Mountains: Five Days

1

teeth chatter in the freezing dawn,
hoarfrost on boulders all round the sleeping bag

morning star
suspended in the brightening sky

sunlight, starlight,
the huge wheel of days

2

black crags
coarse mountain grass
miles of empty sky and stone

a sheep startles –
I watch me pass
through wary yellow eyes:

a cloud of unknowing,
bound up in hoof and horn,
sinew, fleece and bone

3

white sky:
a raven's call
scores a single charcoal mark on emptiness

millennia erode into silence

a sudden small landslip,
a skitter of stones
dislodged from a scree slope

4

midday,
doze on warm stones by a tarn

the waves speak

> I am stone
> I am empty silent mountain air

who invented the wind?

5

coming down to the valley
once again

all those miles of sky and stone

five days
hidden somewhere back up there
between the mountains and the sky

    empty places
    barren places

inexhaustibly fertile

On Trevose Head

he stoops in sunlight,
patterning pebbles
he's brought up from the beach in a sack

it's his day off, and he's making
a mosaic compass
on a high flat place by the lighthouse

beneath a sky
      as blue as a bird's egg,
a high pure lens of air

above a sea
      ruffled to points of white
by a steady south-west wind

he sets his small coloured stones in place

      great-grandfather
      who I never knew

the weight of seventy years of sky
rests
on crumbling concrete and dislodged pebbles.

Wythburn Valley

1

moraine
        blue sky
the valley is an empty trench,
a groove of absent stone

2

pipit's whistle –
flick of a tail by a hummock of moor grass

by the tumbling beck
bird bones half-bedded in peat

we gather white branches to make our fire

3

the sky aches in its sleeve
of earth, grass and stone,
and the beck rings upon emptiness

the valley dreams a cold north wind
to salve the memory in its bones
of the absence of its maker

a chisel of ice betrayed by climate

gravel dumped off its snout in heaps
as it melted back towards its seed,
a single snowflake a million years before

4

we coax flame from ashes
        the next grey misty morning,
and then move on

small travellers
        under a cloudy sky
walking the ghost of a glacier.

Musica Universalis

we have   the spheres   the stars
an ear   ringing   singing
which can hear   in the frosty air the winter of space

Wintering

east wind,
on the sea-wall a hundred gulls
face into it

*

rusty plough,
red hens
scratch in the farmyard

*

dry white grass stalks
rattling,
dark moorland skyline

*

frost all day,
the birds
look twice as big

*

January 1st,
leafless branches,
last year's snow

Crossing the Pass

snow patches
a cairn
a prayer-flag fluent on its bending pole
in a clear high wind from the uplands

crossing the pass
       everything is air and light –
new territory, the first look in
to an unknown land

       high plateau
       the roof of the mind

Hui Neng:

it is neither the flag nor the wind
it is your mind that flaps

Hebridean

tang of drifting peat-smoke
rough grain of sun-warmed granite

I sit in sunlight,
my back against the farmhouse wall,
drinking hot sweet tea
and looking out across the sound to Jura

a snipe
        slowly builds
its huge high tower of air
in a wind like thought itself

then spreads
vibrating tail feathers on the down-swoop

        drumming –
        isn't that what you call it?

the thrum of feathers in
the wind from off the strait

a wind whose name is being here

Gulf Stream

on a northern island,
in a sheltered valley,
an untended garden

the grass-grown bed
of an empty ornamental lake,
mossy gravel paths

rhododendrons gone wild,
azaleas
a blaze of flowers

the air is heavy with fragrance;
in deep foliage
hidden birds call

a micro-climate,
a message
whispered across an ocean

the sea
which can bring such tidings
five thousand miles

Stramongate Bridge, 1 a.m.

the ceiling of the world flows slowly overhead

    rippled clouds
    tide patterns inscribed in sand

the river rushes towards the sea,
wind floods through the trees,
the ruined castle stone by stone
pours itself back into earth

    full moon
    ave regina cœlorum

twenty miles from here
at your behest, beneath your light,
the tide sheets in like clouds
across miles of sand-flats, Morecambe Bay

my head is a high bald hill,
the palm of my hand is a moonlit beach

    fingerprints
    whorls and creases
    lines written on the palm

tide patterns wrinkled in the sand

The Gate

He came a long way round
by steep paths through tangled mountains,
and when at last he came

to the appointed place, he nearly failed
to know it, except that the sunlit path looked
so right for just a moment.

Here he found the riddle of his heart deciphered,
its geography laid out before his eyes
like paradise seen from a hilltop;

here he saw his griefs,
like wisps of smoke from distant chimneys,
dissolving in the placid air;

and, just as his forgotten dream had foretold,
the gate swung open at the sound
of his footfall, admitting him to

a landscape loud with birds, which sang
to tell him that the regime had fallen,
that the lair of power was destroyed for ever.

IV

Hearing the Great Northern Divers Call

1

marsh gentian
cross-leaved heath (or: *bog heather*)
tufted vetch (fern-like leaves, dangling blue flowers)
bog asphodel (a spike of yellow stars)
lousewort (pinkish-purple, clustered wrinkled leaves)
harebells
birdsfoot trefoil (yellow gorse-shaped flowers –
    bacon and eggs, lady's finger, lady's slipper
    fingers and thumbs, Tom Thumb)
tormentil (yellow, four-petalled –
    roots boiled in milk good for diarrhoea)
eyebright (small and white)

2

six ravens,
a pair of peregrine falcons with young

a heronry in old pine trees:
three nests – though one seems deserted –
the adults sit with dignity in the tree tops
or come and go with lazy wing-flaps and trailing legs

the racket of the young (wild, like squealing pigs)
echoes across the water when they're being fed

3

dawn
still water
reeds
a trout jumps
the distant block of Ben Nevis blue in early morning light

mid-morning
chaffinches
a pair of great northern divers
a tree-creeper
goldcrests chipping at the silence among the pines

4

Lochan a' Ghiubhais	:	small loch of the fir tree
Lochan nam Breac	:	small loch of the trout
Lochan an Eisg Mor	:	small loch of the big fish
Lochan Edin	:	small loch of the birds
Lochan na h-Aon Chraoibh	:	small loch of the single tree

5

green mountains
silence
episodic sun and cloud

near a deserted croft
swim in the cold (with sudden warm patches) loch;
peaty water,
wavering limbs a radiant orange-brown

wagtails bob and dip among the lochside boulders
an immature gull sits on a rock in the burn

6

the surface of the loch at evening
blown to confusion by
      veering and backing gusts;
dark sky, downpour, thunderclaps,
lightning makes everything as clear as day

the storm passes into the next valley
      where it roars and flashes
            distantly and more distantly
until midnight
when I go back outside
and hear the great northern divers calling in the dark

Loch Ossian, 4-9 August 1975

Taking the Day Off to Visit the Pound Exhibition

reading *Paterson* on the train to Sheffield

> *the language*
> *the language fails them*
> *they may look at the torrent in their minds*
> *and it is foreign to them*

dark hills above
a sunlit valley green with spring (Edale)

coming out of Totley tunnel,
swaying silver birches,
bluebells,
loamy paths through long wet grass

> *dangerous to leave written that which is badly written:*
> *a chance word, upon paper, may destroy the world*

the train slows as it passes
red-brick terraces under a washed blue sky

in the university library
a poem by Victor Plarr
copied on the fly-leaf of a book owned by Pound

> *oh for it would be a pity*
> *to o'erpraise or to flout her*
> *she was wild, and sweet, and witty*
> *let's not say dull things about her*

(with a later disavowal of interest in Plarr)

> *watch carefully and erase, while*
> *the power is still yours, I say to myself*

first draft of Canto IV, in pencil

> *and beneath it / beneath it / not a ray / not a sliver*
> *not a spare / coin of / sunlight*
> *not a jot / on the / black cold / water*
> *Goddess / Diana / Lucida Sidera*

Dorothy's watercolours of the Pyrenees:
angles, planes and surfaces,
     a pastoral Vorticism,
          off-centre yet nicely balanced –
     no sign of MAXIMUM ENERGY
     or of ALL EXPERIENCE RUSHING INTO THE VORTEX
but 'pleasing to the eye' certainly

first edns. of *Cathay, Lustra, A Draft of XVI Cantos*
the original Canto II with pencilled corrections
a mildewed copy
     of *Cantos XVII–XXVII*
(hidden in a rubbish heap in 1944)

coffee in the Students' Union
     while reading the catalogue:
lads with feet on chairs,
someone sets fire to a plastic cup on a table top
UNION SUBVERSION MEANS FEWER DISCOS – THIS AFFECTS YOU

for all that is put down, once it escapes,
may rot its way into a thousand minds, the corn become
a black smut, and all libraries, of necessity, be
burned to the ground as a consequence

train back through the Pennines,
blown sheets of rain
       in the valley between Hope and Edale,
patches, rays, spare coins of sunlight,
a sudden double rainbow

only one answer:
       write carelessly
so that nothing that is not green will survive

Sheffield, 12 *May* 1976

Looking at the Work Ken Wall Does

a bookcase

top shelf:	a model hippo
	four peanuts
2nd shelf:	a gold-painted Coke bottle
	a small box containing a lead weight on a string
	one raisin
3rd shelf:	an etching block
	a box, PLEASE LOOK: CAREFULLY printed on the lid, containing a fossil snail from the Mesozoic era, 225–265 million years ago, plus the shell of a garden snail and a card explaining that snails live for 4–5 years and are hermaphrodite
4th shelf:	a box of sewing gear
	a small box containing a wrinkled orange
bottom shelf:	a rack of rusty nails

> *I tried to work in a factory, and in an office;*
> *now this is the work I do, it is work which*
> *anyone can do –*
> *not that I want anyone to make work like this,*
> *each can make his own*
> *in his own image*

a trouser-shaped piece of grey canvas with a breech-flap

eight shells stuck to the wall in a *vee* – a flight of wild snails

a pickled bat in a square glass jar

a towel ring with a hank of sheep's wool threaded through it

a hangman's noose

a cobbler's last suspended from a rope

> *if you step outside Western 'reality',
> the nose-to-the-grindstone materialism and rat-race, then
> the* INCIDENT *becomes dominant…*

On the floor the figure of a man half sitting up: between two riding-boot stretchers are two huge rusty iron balls, connected by a rope to the centre of the mirror which is his stomach. Above the mirror, coiled brass tubing and some red and black streamers, and then, at an angle of 45 degrees, a framed X-ray of a rib cage with some small coins glued to it. Above the X-ray, suspended from the ceiling by a rope, an open-sided pine box containing a plaster-of-Paris head with a brass bolt embedded in the centre of the forehead.

> *one thing
> ten thousand things*
> IF UNDELIVERED PLEASE RETURN TO THE BURSAR

step outside

> *the trees are
> very bare
> at this time
> of year*

Newcastle, 30 November 1976

Snow Falling and Then Stopping

I

snow falling all night:
woken twice by
      muffled thumps
as it slides off branches onto the roof

a mid-morning walk:
big, soft flakes float and swirl

sheep in the top field, fleeces
transformed into heavy tasselled skirts by
the lumps of whiteness matted into them,
each animal hesitant, but all behaving
without hesitation as a group

      roll a large
      (larger and larger) snowball down the slope
      to bare some grass for them to eat

the snow stops,
the sun breaks through,
the long ridge of the High Street range,
traversed by the Roman road
      from Brocavum to Galava,
later a packhorse track for peat-cutters
and the site of summer fairs
(wrestling, horse-racing, lost sheep returned to their owners)

shines out against a troubled sky

2

clear today

walk down Correction Hill in sunshine,
the town below, the fallen snow
highlighting planes, angles, the grey of the limestone

  how to make a picture – abstract
  or semi-abstract – that captures
  the shapes, the colour values of this

so a Kendalian seeing it anywhere might think
that reminds me of Kendal
        and be moved
by a cubist configuration
of grey, interlocking, roof-shaped planes
set down just so below a complex angled line –
  the long white ridge of the High Street range
sharp now
against a blue winter sky

Kendal, 31 January–1 February 1977

Watching a Documentary about Eihei-ji, Thinking of Gary Snyder

1

a road through mountains, snow
banked three feet high on either side

dark cedars –
    a dollop of whiteness
slides from a branch, flops to the roadway,
trailing a glimmering crystal cloud behind it

mountains and snow

    if I had a peaceful heart
    it would look like this

the chanting of a sutra in winter stillness,
faint at first but slowly getting louder

2

on each mat a monk,
cross-legged, in a woollen robe

    deep bell, small bell, wooden drum

minus 10°
breath comes out in clouds as they chant

3

4:30 A.M.
feet thump on wooden boards

    a far bell coming closer

a monk sprints through freezing corridors
ringing a hand-bell as he goes

    ice-water in the hand & wash the face

clean the monastery –
    fifteen minutes for
nine hundred metres of wide wooden hallways,
damp cloths
    swept from side to side across
smooth boards as they run

    wipe the feet of the Buddha
    wipe under the bronze incense stands

rice, boiled vegetables, miso soup and pickled radish

4

they step up one by one to ask their question

– what is the Buddha nature like?
– this grain of rice, this snow on the trees

– how about the serpent of passion
   that lies coiled within our hearts?

mountains, cedars,
temple buildings deep in snow

   like a blade which sharpens to nothing

– shine your light on the place where you stand

31 *December* 1977

Hitch-Hiking to Cornwall, Visiting Grandpa in Hospital, Hitch-Hiking Back Again

I

cloudy, warm,
spatters of rain, but clearing later

    wooded richness west of Exeter

a Land Rover, driven by (*what!*) Mick Taylor
now putting his post-Stones band together

    we've toured Britain and Europe,
    but in the autumn we're doing the States –
    that has to be the one

why the Land Rover?

    because it's fun
    because no one argues with it in London
    and because the cottage on Dartmoor's two miles from the road

9 P.M., a roundabout outside Plymouth:
liquid stars
suspended in a dove-grey sky

to Bodmin
with a Londoner working at Wheal Jane

    tin, copper, silver (and in the old days arsenic,
    sulphur, tungsten, zinc, iron and ochre)
    government subsidies just to keep the pumps at work

he and his wife gave notice on the flat in Brixton,
sold the furniture,
put the kids in the back of the car
and drove to Cornwall with £250

> *it worked out all right, but*
> *it could just as easily have gone the other way –*
> *scares me to death when I think about it now*

2

with Eileen to visit Grandpa:
gaunt and frail, helped by a nurse
to where we wait in the visitors' room

> *– how's your chest now, Edwin?*
> *– oh, fine, goat's milk, you know*
> *– goat's milk?*
> *– yes, where do you get yours from?*

he says he's gone deaf
yet can hear Eileen but not me
       (although he recognises me well enough)

difficult silences
watch him turn it over in his head

in the end he shrugs and asks us to leave

3

visit Gladys:
how it was when Grandpa went off his head

>   his delusions,
>   her secret phone-call to the doctor

he tried to leg it
but the ambulance was blocking the gate;
they cornered him by the garage, straight-jacketed him
and carried him kicking away

4

grey dawn,
tamarisk trees, hedges, dunes, grey sea,
a patter of raindrops on the cagoule hood

later: sunshine, grained sand,
sea-smoothed pebbles at the tide-line,
the folded strata of the cliffs

gulls lift off the beach with a little run
and fly out low over incoming waves

5

leave at 7 A.M.
Plymouth to Exeter, an ex-Warrant Officer
(twenty-two years in Coastal Command)

Shackletons:

> *forty-thousand rivets in loose formation*
> *spilling oil all over the world*

he quit because of Nimrod:
     flying jets was too professional,
technology destroyed the crew-spirit
that made it all worthwhile

> *I remember once*
> *we walked down from the base in Singapore*
> *and looked in a tailor-shop window;*
> *the Chinese owner came out and said*
>
>> *– you are aircrew*
>> *– yes, how did you know?*
>> *– ground crew always come alone, aircrew together*
>
> *dead true, although I'd never noticed it myself*
> *and I pride myself on being observant*

a market gardener now and keeps a few pigs

6

leaving Exeter,
a businessman in a Cortina
picks me up, along with a young marine

nineteen years old
and fed up with the service

> 45 *Commando is jungle-trained,*
> 41 *is snow-trained,*
> *but all we're good for is digging trenches on Dartmoor*

he'd been in Ulster and had shot a dog

he'd had a good laugh
when a Catholic who gave them lip
was made to stand in the rain while they took his car to bits

the driver drops him off near Teignmouth

> *hard as nails, that boy,*
> *hard as nails, he'd smile while he killed you,*
> *they're quite superb – I know a lot of those lads –*
> *and technically so good*

7

    eleven hours at Gordano Services

        so boring, so frustrating
        that in the end it becomes interesting again

    an ex-India traveller, an ex-squaddie,
        a youth-worker from Moss Side,
    a roundabout, a roadside, cups of tea in the café,
    hours and hours
    with thumb raised to a stream of unrelenting traffic

        and then
        at last
        at 11 P.M.

    a lift from two Scousers in a Transit
    all the way to Knutsford

A38, *St Merryn,* & M5: 14–18 *May* 1978

Starting the Day

> *'Kendal Mint Cake is still made in exactly the same way as it was nearly* 100 *years ago, stirring the sugar by hand in copper pans to get that magic taste'*

7:45 A.M.

    roll out of bed,
    shave, dress,
    pad through to the kitchen,
    toast and tea standing by the stove

out, the trees around the bungalow
green and stately in early morning light

    dew on roadside grasses,
    cattle browse in fields below,
    mist patches on limestone heights,
    sheep's wool snagged on barbed wire fences

wet boots and jean-bottoms swish downhill
to the stone-built town in its cradle of fells

newspaper and a cup of tea in the café
and then to work
Wilson's, Producers of Quality Confectionery, Estd. 1913

    morning, Fred
    morning, Andrew
    morning, Paul

open doors and windows to let in light and air
put a match to the pilot lights, heave
the copper boiling-pan onto the slow burner
a gallon of water from the steel bucket
a teaspoon and a half of salt
fetch the stirring stick, coax
the hardened sugar mixture from the bottom of the pan
23 lbs of sugar
carry it across the room, cascade it into the water

another 23 lbs, then stir it in with the stick

> the
> only
> sound
> the
> quiet
> hiss
> of the
> pilot
> lights

a shout to Fred
together carry the pan to the fast burner
(it starts with a roar as he presses the button)

run hot water over the thermometer bulb
see the mercury rise
turn it upside down, give it a tap and watch
a sliver of quicksilver slide the length of the tube
(picking up stray mercury fragments as it goes)

turn it right way up, check
the sliver rejoins the mercury in the bulb
put the thermometer in the bucket
(with stirring sticks, sieves, knives and scrapers)

8:45: the first hour's done, the day's begun

Kendal, 14 August 1978

V

Du Fu

after Armand Robin

more than a thousand years ago
in the timeless world of song

away from myself and my life
I met Du Fu

far from any country, any time,
we were friends in an instant

he steadied my unstable craft
he was harder on me than myself

deeper than water
he was my most harrowing moments

in the ruins of Chang-an I found my homeland
I fled with him from village to village

he had borne
massacre   ruin   war

who should he try to please?

Seeing Sights in Sanctuary Wood

Hill 62, Ypres Salient

among saplings and new leaves, tree-stumps
pock-marked with the bullets of sixty years ago

> broken rifles,
> split gas-canisters,
> dented helmets, shell cases

the muddy-bottomed trench –
five feet deep, the firing-step supported
> by rusted corrugated-iron –
zigzags for fifty yards to the edge of the wood

beyond the fence, a field
ploughed level now, green with corn

> a tractor working somewhere,
> a distant grumble
> filtering through April birdsong

on tables inside the museum
polished wooden boxes
two eyeholes on the front and a handle on the side,
3-D photographs, thirty or forty to a box:

legless, armless, headless, corpses in mud;
bones protrude
> through blackened flesh or tattered cloth;
a skeleton's hand grasps a rifle,
the top half of a skull
two feet from the rest of the head

shell-shocked men
stare at us and into a far, dark distance
as they stared
through and beyond the man with the camera

five soldiers sit in a shell-hole having a smoke;
two men, tunics open, boots off,
    eat a loaf of bread in the sun;
a soldier walks a greasy duckboard through
    the oceanic mud of Passchendaele

soldiers of the Great War, known unto God

the souvenir shop offers
guidebooks, postcards, mugs, statuettes, plaques,
polished brass cartridges
and ashtrays made from sawn-off shell-cases

The Temptation of St Anthony

Hieronymous Bosch

this one has a pig snout and cunning eyes
he holds out his cup for wine
an owl is perched on his head

this one wears a bishop's robes
blood pours from his back
he disputes a sacred text with a bird and a fish

this one is obsequious
he carries a frog on a silver platter
the frog also carries a platter

this one is serious
he wears a tall black hat
a blackbird's claw sticks out from under his cloak

this one has no arms
he is up to his waist in water
a bowl of porridge is balanced on his head

this one is naked
he blows a trumpet
a sausage pops out on a string

and here is a pig
an earthen pitcher
which pisses from its bunghole

and here is Mr Burgher
with his missus
riding complacently through the sky on a fish

over here is a burning town
and these are the winged devils
who wheel among the flames

over there is a marching army
this here is a gibbet
and these are human bones scattered on the ground

but who is this
cloaked and bearded figure
the still point at the hub of this demented mandala?

just one more figure in a sea of hallucination
but the only one who looks us in the eye
mon semblable, mon frère, he stares straight out at us

his eyes are haunted
unexpectant
with just a trace of mockery

and even though he
long ago finished with questions,
his eyes ask

do you also see truly
are you also a witness?

www.ingramcontent.com/pod-product-compliance
Lightning Source LLC
Chambersburg PA
CBHW031208090426
42736CB00009B/838